A New True Book

COYOTES

By Emilie U. Lepthien

CP CHILDRENS PRESS®
CHICAGO

Coyote

PHOTO CREDITS

© Reinhard Brucker—28

H. Armstrong Roberts—© McKinney, 13 (right);
© T. Ulrich, 20 (left), 25

Photri—5 (left)

Root Resources—© Franz J. Camenzind, 11, 29, 30, 32, 33 (bottom), 35, 38, 42; © Diana Stratton, 14

Tom Stack & Associates—© Thomas Kitchin, 2; © W. Perry Conway, 10 (left), 13 (left); © Victoria Hurst, 16; © Jeff Foott, 40; © Richard P. Smith, 41

Tony Stone, Worldwide/Chicago—© Tom Ulrich, 15, 18; © Leonard Lee Rue III, 22; © Gary Bumgarner, 33 (top)

SuperStock International, Inc.—© Three Lions, 8

Valan—© Stephen J. Krasemann, Cover, 21 (right); © Dennis W. Schmidt, 5 (right), 17, 20 (right), 23, 27, 36; © Jeff Foott, 10 (right), 21 (left); © Wayne Lankinen, 43

Visuals Unlimited—© Ron Spomer, 6; © Wm. Grenfell, 7, 19; © Leonard Lee Rue III, 39; © Stephen J. Lang, 44; © John S. Flannery, 45

Cover—Coyote

Project Editor: Fran Dyra
Design: Margrit Fiddle

To the members of Beta Alpha Chapter,
The Delta Kappa Gamma Society International

Library of Congress Cataloging-in-Publication Data

Lepthien, Emilie U. (Emilie Utteg)
  Coyotes / by Emilie U. Lepthien.
    p.   cm. — (A New true book)
  Includes index.
  Summary: Discusses the physical characteristics, habits, range, diet, and social nature of coyotes.
  ISBN 0-516-01331-9
  1. Coyotes—Juvenile literature.
[1. Coyotes.] I. Title.
QL737.C22L483   1993
599.74'442—dc20   92-35050
                                            CIP
                                             AC

TABLE OF CONTENTS

"THE TRICKSTER"

The Navajo called the coyote "little brother." The Plains people named the clever coyote "The Trickster."

Coyotes play tricks. They trick other animals and people, too. They move silently. Suddenly, they appear in the open. Just as suddenly they disappear into brush or woodlands.

The coyote in this Aztec stone statue (left)
sits just like a real coyote (above).

The Aztecs of Mexico
called the animal *coyotl.* The
Spanish explorers changed
that to *coyote.* Now coyote is
the animal's common name.

5

WHAT IS A COYOTE?

Wolves, coyotes, jackals, and dogs are related. They are all descended from a doglike animal called

A coyote hunting its prey moves very much like a dog.

Tomarctus that lived over
one million years ago.

Coyotes belong to the
family Canidae. Their
scientific name is *Canis
latrans,* which means
"barking dog."

Coyotes are mammals.
Their young—called pups—are 7

Coyote pups

born alive. The mother feeds
the pups with her milk.

Coyotes are mainly
carnivores, or meat eaters,
but sometimes they eat
plants. They are predators.
They catch and kill animals

for food.

POPULATION AND RANGE

The Spanish explorers found coyotes in Mexico 400 years ago. Coyotes lived on the Great Plains when Lewis and Clark explored the West almost 200 years ago.

Now they can be found in the Middle West and the northeastern United States. Coyotes also live in Alaska and in western and southern Canada. They have spread as far south as Panama in Central America.

Woodlands (above) and grasslands
(right) are good homes for coyotes.

Coyotes prefer to live in
open grasslands and the
edges of woodlands. There
are probably more coyotes
today than there were when
the first settlers arrived. The
coyote population may total
1.5 million.

Coyotes have adapted well to different climates and new areas. They like to live near farms and ranches. Frequently, they are seen in towns and cities.

A coyote visits a swimming pool in Hollywood, California.

HUNTING FOR PREY

Coyotes usually hunt at night. Their keen senses of hearing and smell are important for hunting.

They often hunt alone, but sometimes they hunt in pairs. One coyote acts as a decoy while the other one stays hidden. Usually, mates form a hunting pair.

Coyote (left) digs into a
prairie dog burrow. Prairie dogs (above)
live in "towns" that contain
hundreds of underground burrows.

Coyotes hunt small
rodents. Prairie dogs, mice,
and rabbits are the coyotes'
favorite foods. But they also
eat insects, berries, nuts,
and fruits.

Coyotes and badgers
sometimes work together to

Badgers dig with their strong front feet and long claws.

find food. Badgers are slow-moving, but they can dig very fast. When a badger digs into a prairie dog burrow, a coyote will stand nearby.

When a prairie dog dashes out of the burrow, it could escape the slow-moving badger—but not the

Coyotes sometimes eat the dead meat they find.
This elk died during the harsh winter.

fast-moving coyote. Soon
the badger and the coyote
are sharing a meal.

Sometimes a pack of ten
or more coyotes may bring
down a deer or an elk. When
two or more coyotes hunt
together, they share the catch. **15**

Coyote raiding a chicken coop on a farm

FRIEND AND FOE

When none of their favorite foods are available, coyotes may hunt chickens, sheep, and lambs. This angers farmers and ranchers. Coyotes also raid garbage cans.

Coyote hunting a deer mouse

But Coyotes help farmers
by eating the rodents that
feed on farmers' crops. They
also help ranchers. Rodents
eat the grasses on which
domestic animals graze.
There would not be enough
grass for sheep and cattle if

coyotes did not hunt rodents. Coyotes also eat carrion—animals that are already dead. They help to clean up the environment by getting rid of carrion.

Coyote carries off the head of an elk.

Coyote caught in a trap

ENEMIES

Humans are probably the
coyote's main enemies today.
Poisons, traps, guns, and
dogs are used to reduce
the coyote population.

19

The bobcat (above) is much smaller than its cousin the cougar (right).

In the wild, coyotes' enemies include wolves, bears, and cougars. Coyotes and bobcats are fierce enemies. Coyotes will drive bobcats up trees, and wait to catch them when they come down.

The red wolf (above) and the timber wolf (right) are related to coyotes.

A SMALL ANIMAL

Coyotes are smaller than their relatives the timber wolves and red wolves. They stand 2 feet tall at the shoulder. They are about 3 feet long. Their bushy tails are 1 to 1½ feet long. They have long legs and small feet like a dog's.

Coyotes have long legs that help them run fast.

Coyotes have slender
bodies that are well suited to
running fast. They weigh
between 25 and 50 pounds.
Wolves are two to three
times their size.

Coyotes run with their tail
between their legs. Wolves
run with their tail curled over

their back. A running coyote can change direction quickly. Then its tail acts like a rudder. The tail helps the animal keep its balance while turning.

Coyotes can leap 12 feet to pounce on a fleeing rodent. They can also swim when necessary.

Coyote pounces on a mouse.

CHANGING COATS

Most coyotes are grayish brown with reddish flanks. Their feet and legs are tawny colored. Those living in the far north have lighter-colored but heavier coats than those living farther south.

The color of their coat changes with the seasons. The guard hairs are darker in

The coyote's thick winter coat is lIghter in color than its summer coat.

summer and lighter in winter.
In winter, their soft, warm
underfur is thicker. The layer
of guard hairs sheds rain
and snow.

The coyote's black nose quivers when it picks up a new odor.

Their black, leatherlike nose pad is smaller than a wolf's. Their nose quivers when they pick up a new odor.

Coyotes' eyes are yellowish and slightly slanted. They look very

28

Coyote eats a bison (buffalo) that died during the winter in Yellowstone Park.

bright and alert, but their vision is poor. They can see only movement, not details.

Coyotes have 42 teeth. The teeth are good for grasping, holding, and tearing their prey.

A male and a female coyote; coyote pairs sometimes mate for life.

COYOTE FAMILIES

Coyote pairs stay together for at least a year. Some pairs mate for life. They mate in late winter or early spring. Two months later the pups are born. Usually there are 4 to 7 pups in a litter. However, as many as 19 pups have been counted.

The female coyote prepares

These tiny coyote pups are only two days old.

a den to use when the pups
are born. Sometimes the
male helps in digging out
a den.

For the first two weeks
after birth the pups feed
on their mother's milk. She
stays in the den with them,
leaving only for short periods

When the pups are a little older they may try to leave the den (above).
A mother coyote (below) nurses her litter.

to feed. The father has his own den nearby. He guards his mate's den and the litter of pups.

The female gives food to the pups even while they are still nursing. At first, she feeds them regurgitated, partially digested, food. Later, she brings them small bones to chew. This strengthens their jaw muscles.

Coyote pups take a peek at the outside world from their den entrance.

NEW DENS

The pups stay in the den for two months. They may peek out occasionally. The mother may move them to another den. One den may have too many fleas that bother her and her litter.

Young coyotes explore the world around their den.

Before moving the pups into the new, clean den, the mother rolls each pup in the grass to rub off the fleas.

Wherever they are, the father patrols on guard duty. He protects his mate and their litter from enemies.

FATHER AND TEACHER

The pups meet their father
when they are two months
old. He leads them out of the
den for their first hunting
lesson. He teaches them to
catch grasshoppers. Later
he teaches them to catch
field mice and other small
rodents.

This coyote family has made their den in the middle of a large grassy field.

Before long, the pups hunt with their parents. To find food, the family often travels far from their dens.

The parents protect their young for almost a year. By then the pups are almost full grown.

COMMUNICATING

Like many wild animals, coyotes mark their territory with urine or musk. The odor warns other coyotes to stay out of their territory.

After sunset, coyotes can be heard howling. Howling is one way of communicating.

Coyote howling

It is often hard to tell where a coyote's howl is coming from. They can trick other animals or people into thinking they are in a different place.

They throw their head back and begin with a "yap-yap" sound. The sound quickly changes to a long, eerie howl. The note is very high-pitched. Soon other coyotes join in. They sometimes howl during the day. They also bark, growl, and wail to communicate.

Coyotes roll in the grass to leave their special scent.

Coyotes have other ways of communicating, too. Each coyote has a slightly different odor. A strong scent comes from a gland at the base of the tail. They can tell by the smell whether another coyote is a friend or an enemy.

In winter, coyotes hunt rodents that burrow under the snow.

SURVIVORS

Coyotes survive because they have adapted to the changes in their environment.

People have tried many ways to control the coyote population. But coyotes are very clever. They know how

Young coyotes play together to develop
the skills they need for hunting.

to eat the bait in a trap
without being caught.
Coyotes are survivors.
During the last century, they
have moved throughout North
America. Their population
continues to grow.

WORDS YOU SHOULD KNOW

adapt (uh • DAPT)—adjust, change

badger (BAD • jer)—an animal with a thick body and short legs

burrow (BER • oh)—a hole that an animal digs in the ground to make a home

carnivore KAR • nih • vore)—an animal that eats meat

Carrion (KAR • ee • yun)—dead animals used for food

climate (KLY • mit)—the kind of weather that usually occurs at a certain place

communicate (kuh • MYOO • nih • kayt)—to pass information back and forth

coyote (KYE • oht)—a wild animal that looks like a small wolf

decoy (DEE • koy)—a thing that is used to lure someone into a trap

den (DEN)—an animal's home

domestic (doh • MESS • tik)—kept and cared for by people

eerie (EER • ee)—strange and spooky; weird

environment (en • VY • run • ment)—the things that surround a plant or an animal; the lands and waters of the earth

explorer (ex • PLOR • er)—a person who travels to far-off places to learn about the land and the people there

gland (GLAND)—a special body part that makes materials that the body can use or give off

guard hairs (GARD HAIRZ)—long hairs in the outer fur of animals

litter (LIT • er)—a group of baby animals born at the same time from the same mother

mammal (MAM • il)—one of a group of warm-blooded animals that have hair and nurse their young with milk

musk (MUHSK)—a substance with a strong and lasting odor

population (pop • yoo • LAY • shun)—the total number of animals of the same kind living at the same time

predator (PREH • di • ter) — an animal that hunts other animals for food

prey (PRAY) — an animal that is hunted and eaten by another animal

range (RAINJ) — the region in which a certain plant or animal can be found in the wild

regurgitated (re • GER • jih • tay • tid) — swallowed and then brought back up

rodent (ROH • dint) — an animal that has long, sharp front teeth for gnawing

rudder (RUH • der) — a movable finlike structure placed at the rear of a boat to help in steering

tawny (TAW • nee) — brownish yellow

territory (TAIR • ih • tor • ree) — an area with definite boundaries that an animal lives in

trickster (TRICK • ster) — one who likes to play tricks on others

INDEX

About the Author

Emilie U. Lepthien received her BA and MS degrees and certificate in school administration from Northwestern University. She taught upper-grade science and social studies, wrote and narrated science programs for the Chicago Public Schools' station WBEZ, and was principal in Chicago, Illinois, for twenty years. She received the American Educator's Medal from Freedoms Foundation.

She is a member of Delta Kappa Gamma Society International, Chicago Principals' Association, Illinois Women's Press Association, National Federation of Press Women, and AAUW.

She has written books in the Enchantment of the World, New True Books, and America the Beautiful series.